Numbers 0-20 Wipe-Clean Activity Book

for ages 3-5

This CGP wipe-clean book is full of colourful number activities for Pre-School and Reception children.

It's a fun way to introduce the essential skills — and you can wipe it clean to enjoy again and again!

Helpful Hints

- Use the pen provided to write or draw your answers.
  You can practise the numbers as many times as you want to.
  Just wipe the pen away once you have finished the page and have another go.

- Keep the pen away from your eyes. Avoid getting the ink on clothing, furniture or fabric as it may not be washable.

- A grown-up can help you read the questions.
  Let them know which activities you enjoy the most.

- Find a nice place to work.
  Make sure you're comfortable at your desk or table.

- Writing the numbers nice and clearly is really important.
  Work neatly, and try to keep your pen inside the lines.

- 'Tony's Treasure Hunt' in the centre covers the numbers 0-20
  — you may want to save this until last.

Published by CGP
ISBN: 978 1 78908 969 1

Editors: Duncan Lindsay and Gabrielle Richardson.

With thanks to Keith Blackhall and Gareth Mitchell for the proofreading.
With thanks to Alice Dent for the copyright research.

Printed by Elanders Ltd, Newcastle upon Tyne.

Cover and graphics used throughout the book © Educlips
Cover design concept by emc design ltd.

Text, design, layout and original illustrations
© Coordination Group Publications Ltd. (CGP) 2023
All rights reserved.

CGP, Broughton House, Griffin Street,
Broughton-in-Furness, Cumbria, LA20 6HH

CGP c/o Elanders GmbH, Anton-Schmidt-Str. 15,
71332 Waiblingen, GERMANY

Photocopying this book is not permitted, even if you have a CLA licence.
Extra copies are available from CGP with next day delivery • 0800 1712 712 • www.cgpbooks.co.uk

Contents

The Numbers 0 to 2	2
The Numbers 3 to 5	4
The Numbers 6 to 8	6
The Numbers 9 and 10	8
Tony's Treasure Hunt	10
Ordering Numbers 0 to 10	12
The Numbers 11 to 13	14
The Numbers 14 to 16	16
The Numbers 17 to 20	18
Ordering Numbers 11 to 20	20
Odd and Even Numbers	22

The Numbers 0 to 2

First Try This

Trace the numbers below with your pen.

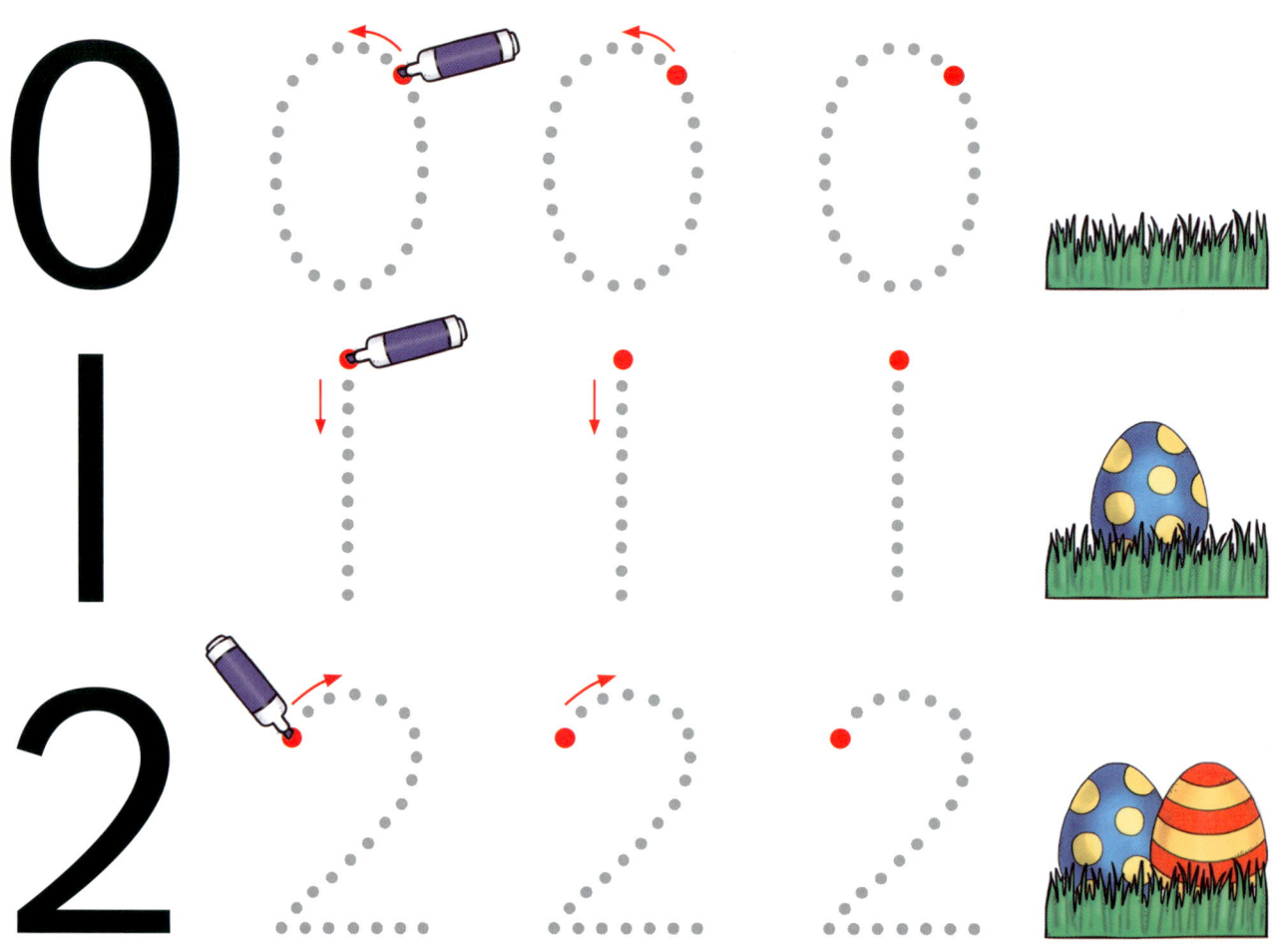

Now Try These

Circle each nest that has 1 bird in it.

Trace the numbers in the boxes to complete the sentences.

There is  rabbit.

The rabbit has  carrots.

The rabbit has  ears.

Draw lines to match the pictures to the right number of bugs.

0   1   2

Circle all the gnomes.

How many gnomes did you circle?
Write your answer in the box.

Well done! You know all about 0, 1 and 2. Draw a smiley face.

The Numbers 3 to 5

First Try This

Trace the numbers below with your pen.

3 3 3 3

4 4 4 4

5 5 5 5

Now Try These

Tick the boxes next to the cakes that have 4 candles.

Trace the lollipops to complete the picture. How many lollipops are there in total? Circle your answer.

3
4
5

Trace the numbers in the boxes. Draw lines to match each number to the right picture.

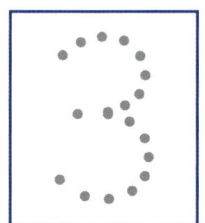   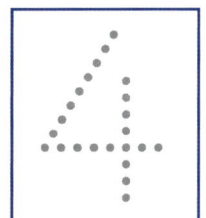   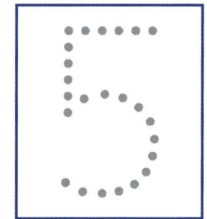

Draw sweets so there are the right number in each jar.

Wow, you've mastered 3, 4 and 5! Draw a smiley face.

The Numbers 6 to 8

First Try This

Trace the numbers below with your pen.

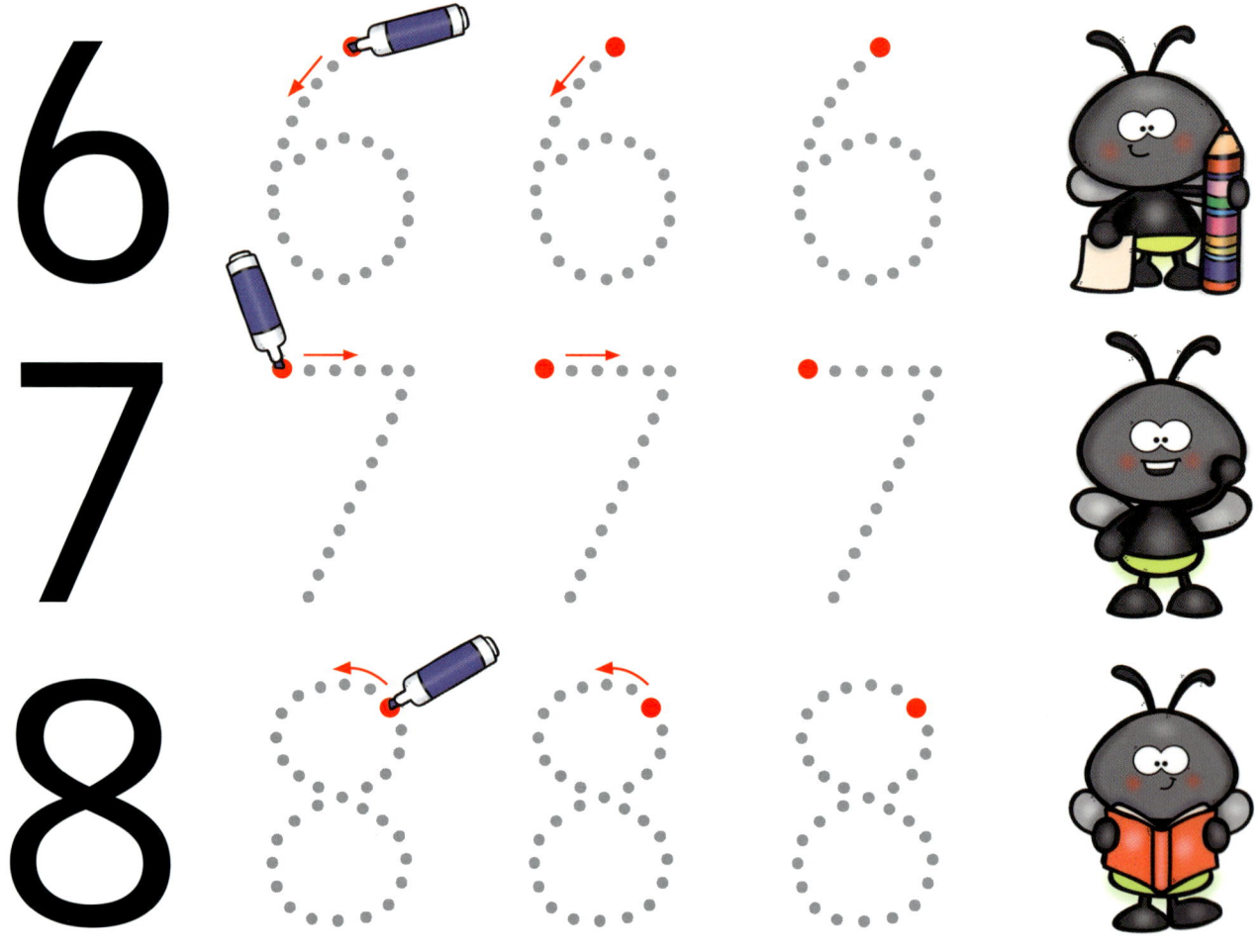

Now Try These

Circle all the ants that are carrying the number 8.

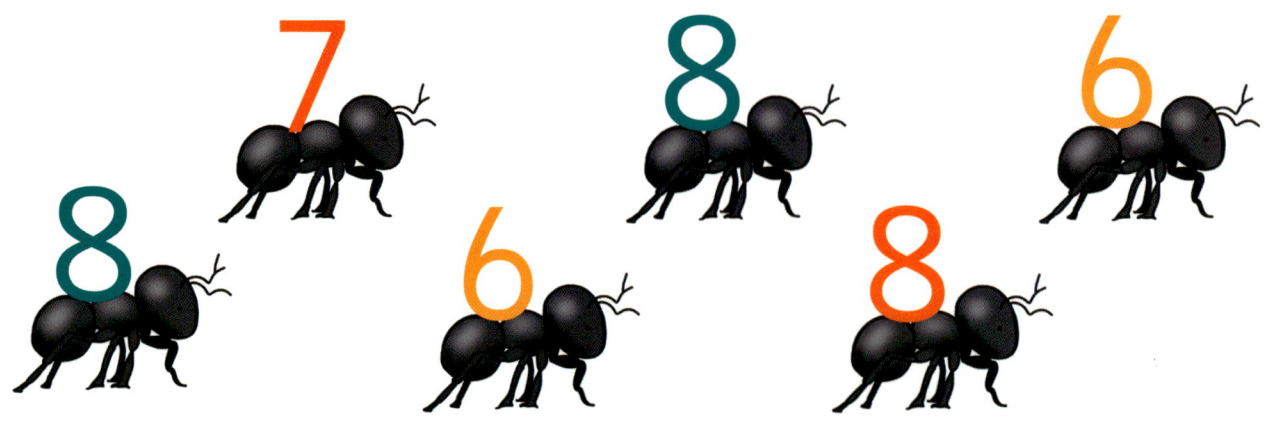

Draw the right number of spots on the bugs.

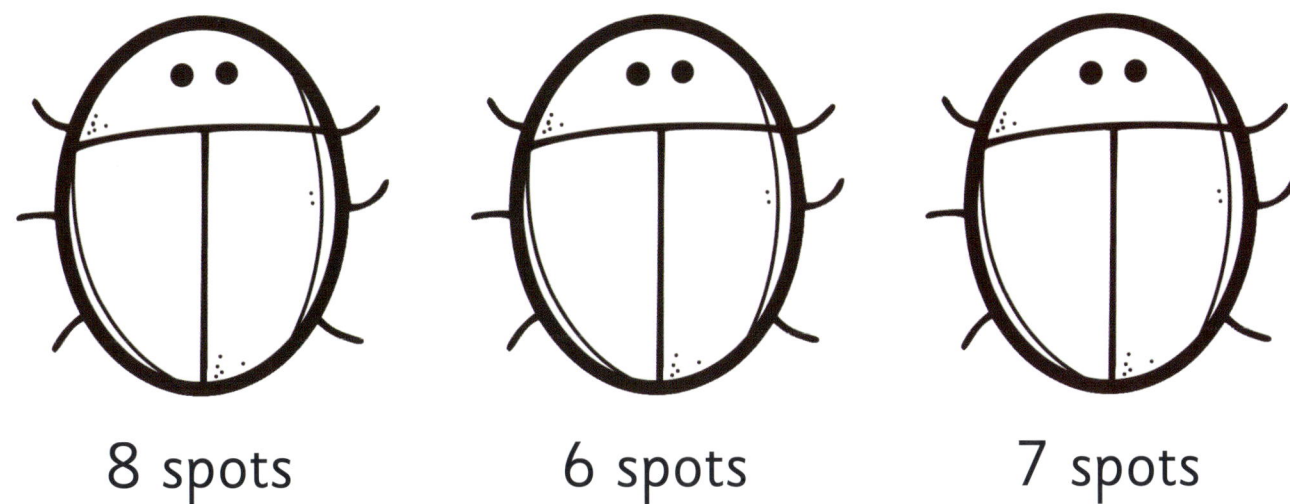

8 spots   6 spots   7 spots

Trace the legs on the spider to complete the picture.

How many legs does the spider have? Circle your answer.

6   7   8

How many bees are there? Write the number in the box.

You've done a great job with 6, 7 and 8! Draw a smiley face.

The Numbers 9 and 10

First Try This

Trace the numbers below with your pen.

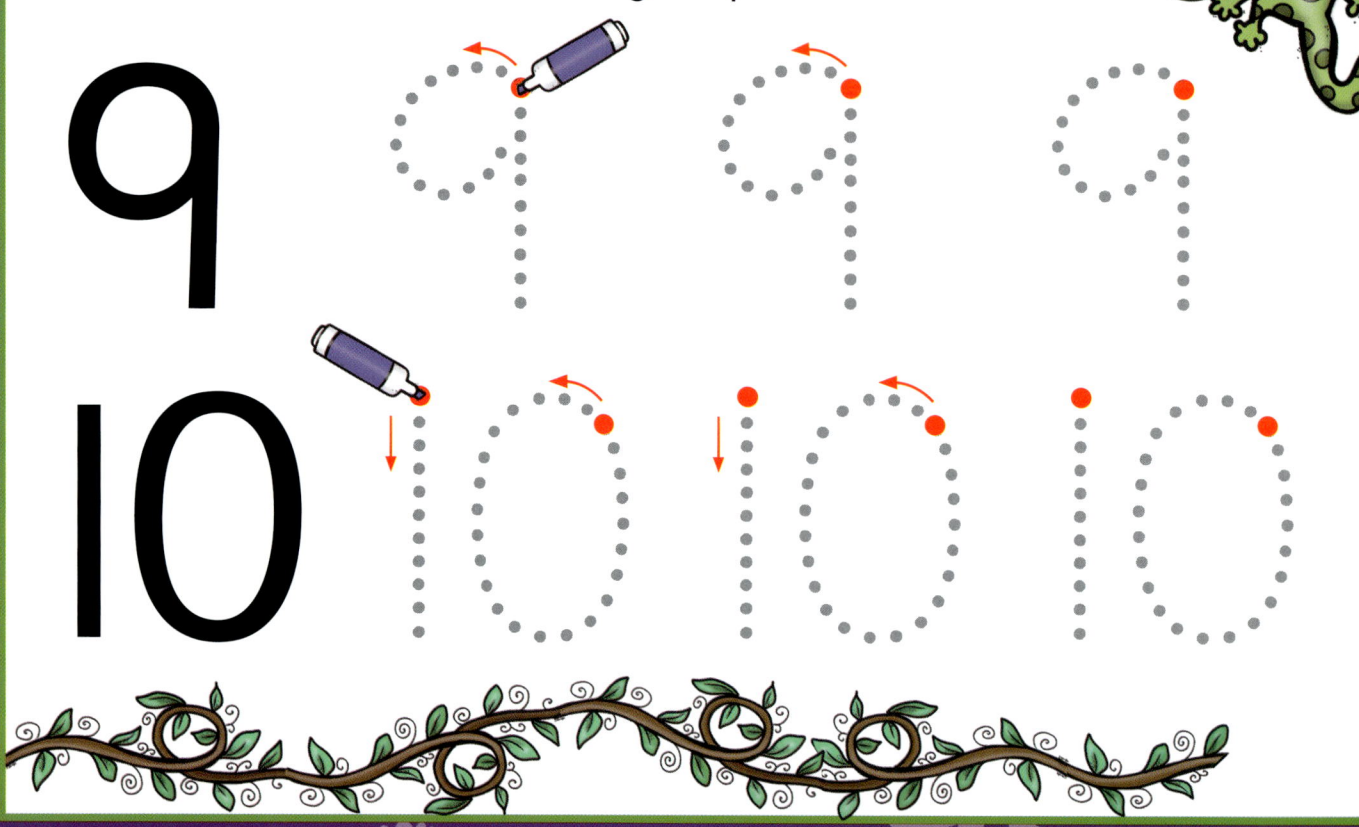

Now Try These

Draw lines so that all of the beads with a number 10 are joined up.

How many 9 and 10 beads are there in total? Write your answer in the box.

Trace the apples to complete the picture.

How many apples are there in total?
Write your answer in the box.

Draw a line from each sheep with a number 9 to the barn.

Wonderful! You've learned about 9 and 10. Draw a smiley face.

Tony's Treasure Hunt

Solve the clues and write your answers in the boxes. Then, trace the shapes in the picture that contain your answers to reveal where the treasure is hidden.

How many balloons is Shanice holding?

Count all the balls in the machines. How many are there?

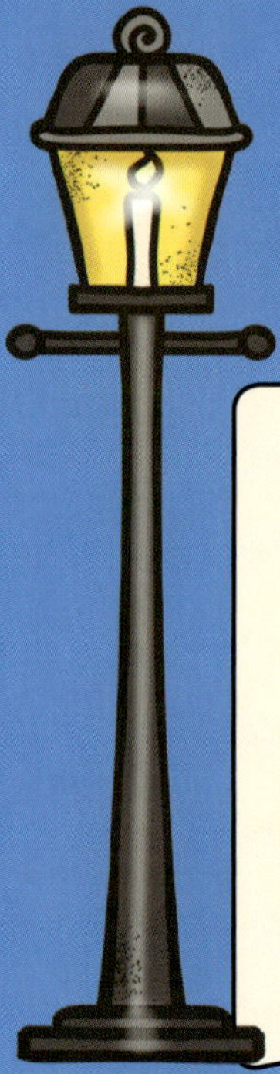

Circle all the odd numbers below. How many numbers have you circled?

2   9   6
7   4   5   8

Which shape has the numbers in the right order?
Draw the shape in the box.

7 3 9

9 10 11

15 16 12

Circle all the even numbers below.
How many numbers have you circled?

8   6   7   10
  3   2   4

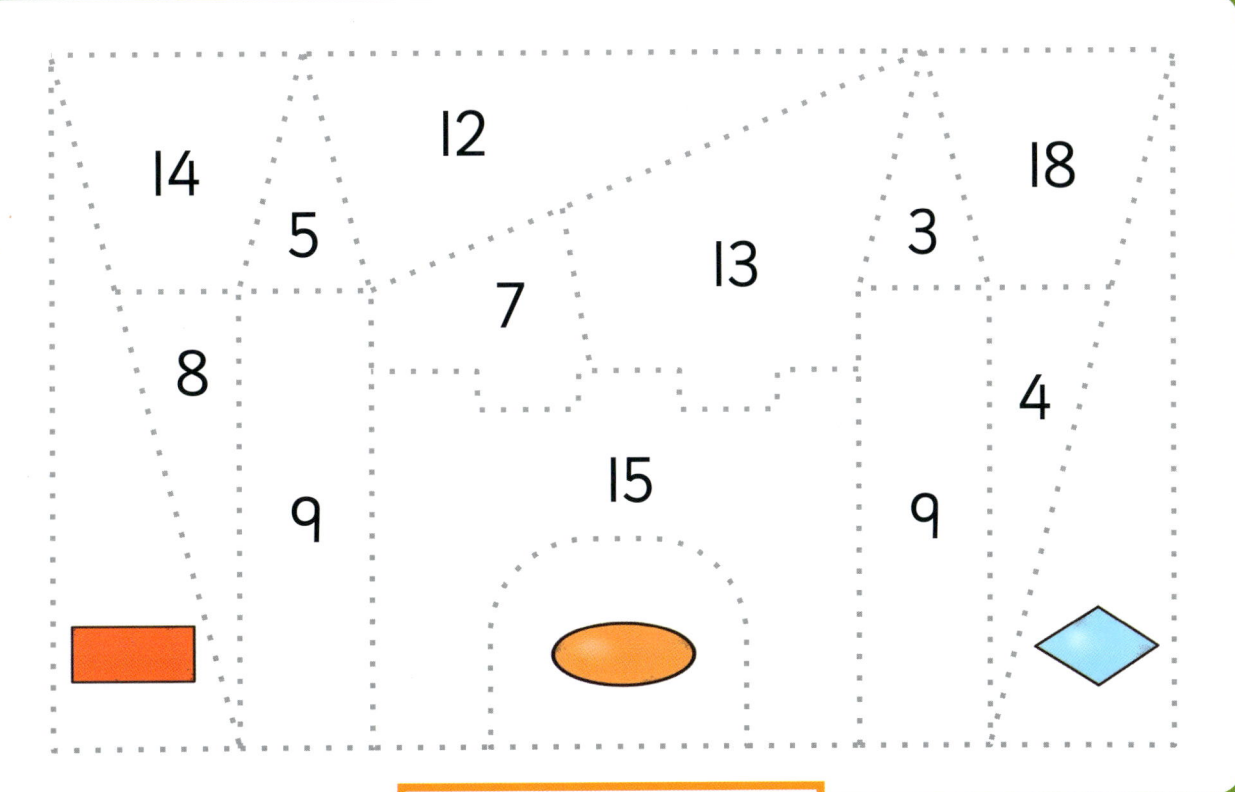

What can you see?

Ordering Numbers 0 to 10

First Try This

A number line shows you a line of numbers in the right order.

0 1 2 3 4 5 6 7 8 9 10

Trace the numbers below with your pen to complete the number lines.

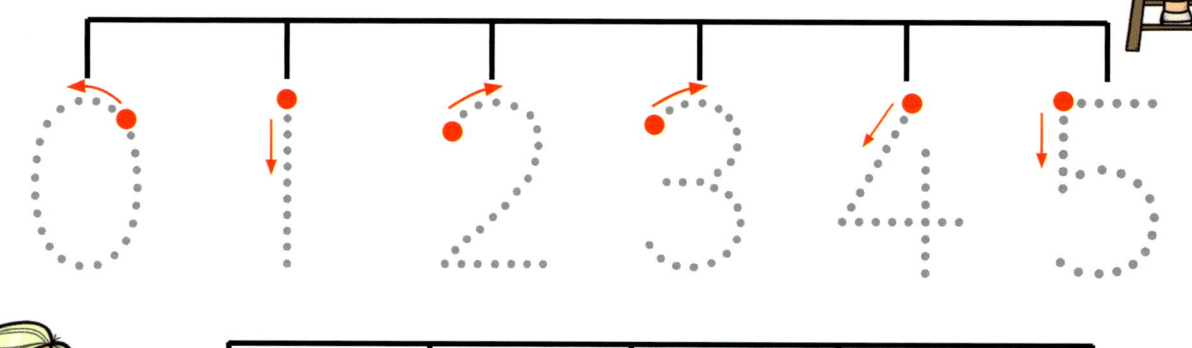

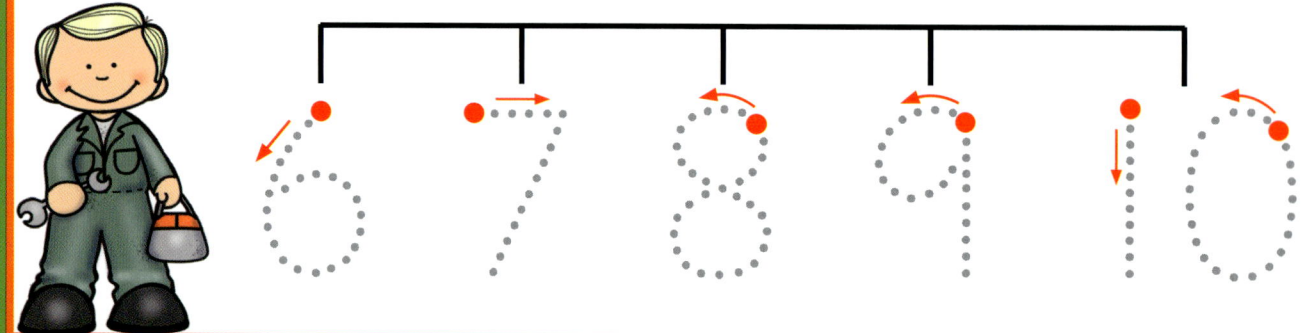

Now Try These

Draw lines to connect the numbers in the right order.

Draw lines to put the numbers in the right places in the line of mugs.

2   3   1   5

Trace the numbers below with your pen to complete the sentences.

The number 5 comes one before 6.

The number 10 comes one after 9.

Fill in the gaps in the number line.

Amazing! You've put everything in order. Draw a smiley face.

The Numbers 11 to 13

First Try This

Trace the numbers below with your pen.

11
12
13

Now Try These

Trace the numbers to complete the picture.

Circle all the fish that show the number 13.

How many frogs are there? Write the number in the box.

Draw more raindrops so that there are 11 in total below the clouds.

How many raindrops would there be if you drew 2 more? Write your answer in the box.

Superb! You've done really good work. Draw a smiley face.

The Numbers 14 to 16

First Try This

Trace the numbers below with your pen.

14 14 14
15 15 15
16 16 16

Now Try These

Circle all the children holding the number 15.

How many eyes do the monsters have in total?
Write your answer in the box.

Draw more beans so that there are 16 beans in total.

Draw lines to match the shopping to the right trolley.
Circle any shopping that does not match either trolley.

Yippee! You've done really well! Draw a smiley face.

The Numbers 17 to 20

First Try This

Trace the numbers below with your pen.

17　17　17
18　18　18
19　19　19
20　20　20

Now Try These

How many marbles are there? Write your answer in the box.

Draw lines so that all of the counters with a number 19 are joined up.

Draw dots on the blank dice so there are 20 dots in total.

Write the missing numbers on the cards so they match the descriptions below.

Wow, you've learnt the numbers up to 20! Draw a smiley face.

Ordering Numbers 11 to 20

First Try This

You can put the numbers 11-20 in the right order on a number line.

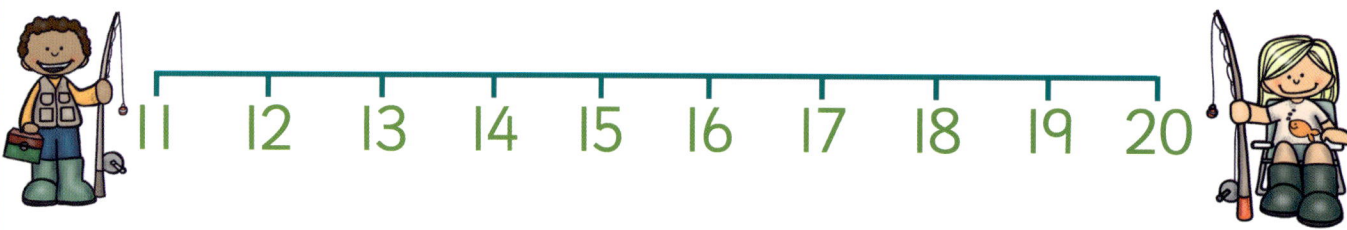

Trace the numbers on the number lines with your pen.

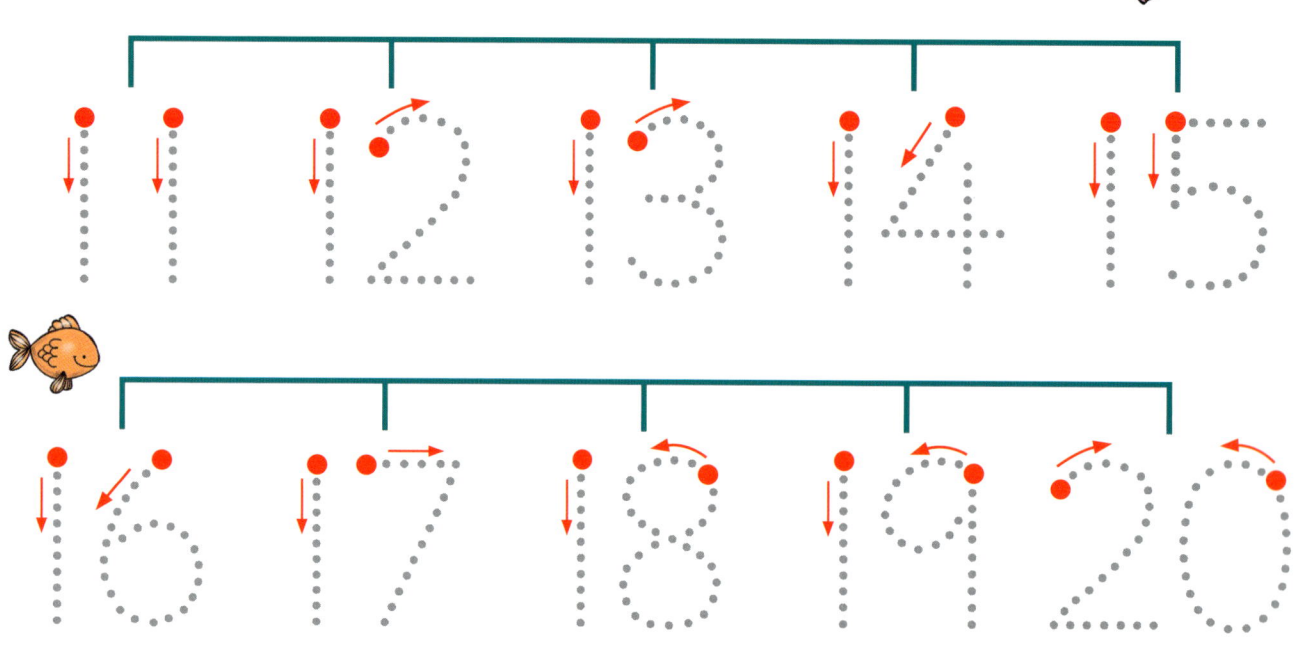

Now Try These

Which number is missing from the number line?
Write your answer in the box.

Circle each fruit that has a number between 13 and 17 on it.

Trace around the snake with the numbers in the right order.

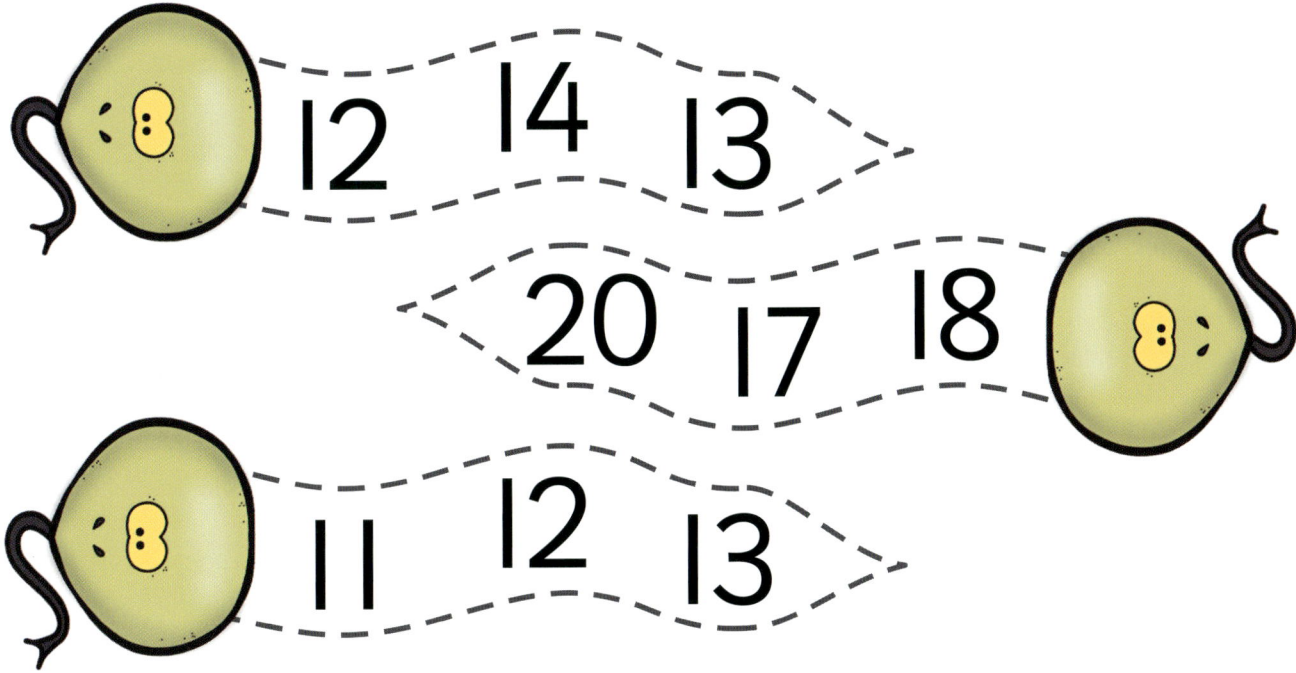

Write these numbers in the right order on the train.

20   18   19

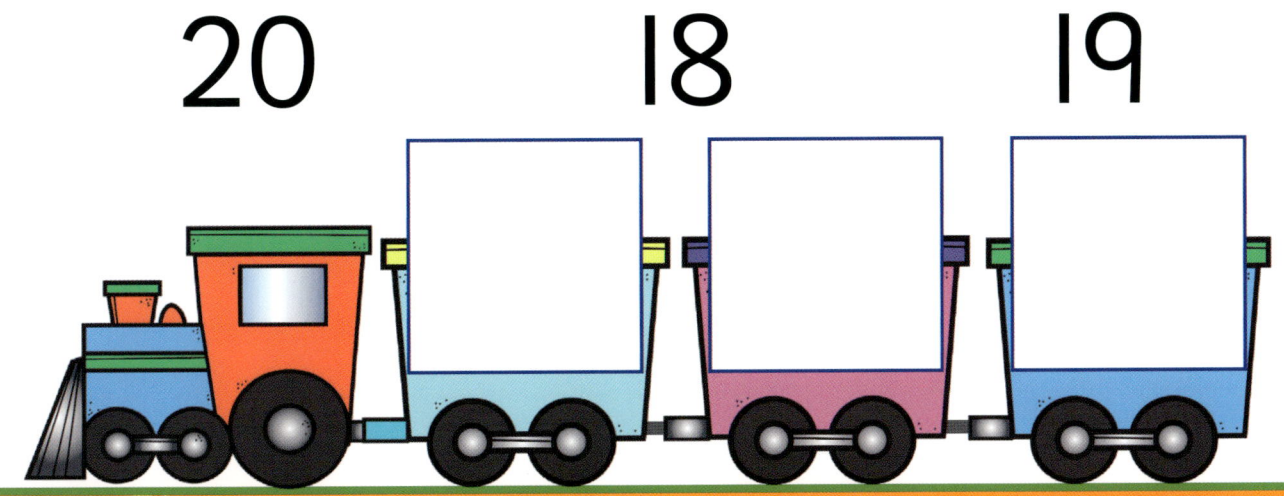

Fab! You know all about ordering numbers. Draw a smiley face.

Odd and Even Numbers

First Try This

These numbers are **odd**:   1   3   5   7   9

These numbers are **even**:   2   4   6   8   10

Trace the odd numbers. Circle the even numbers.

1   2   3   6   9

Now Try These

Draw lines from each number to show if it is odd or even.

Trace around all the shapes with even numbers.

8   10   7   2   5

Woohoo! You can sort odd and even numbers. Draw a smiley face.